MW01229342

MORE

African

PROVERBS

Published by

POCKET GIFTS

An Imprint of BOOKCRAFT LTD.
29, Moremi Road, New Bodija
P. O. Box 16279, Ibadan
Tel/Fax:(02)8103238
Email: oziengbe@skannet.com

in association with
LADY ADEMOLA
4b, Ilado Close, Ikoyi, Lagos.

UK & USA Distributors:
African Books Collective
The Jam Factory
27, Park End Street,
Oxford, Ox1 1HU, UK
Tel: +44(0)1865-726686
Fax: +44(0)1865-793298
Email: abc@dial.pipex.com
website:africanbookscollective.com

ISBN: 978-2030-94-5

Layout and Design: Dupe Olayebi
Cover Design: Biodun Adeogun

PREFACE

THE FIRST COMPILATION OF AFRICAN PROVERBS SELECTED FROM THE BBC OVERSEAS SERVICE HAS BEEN SO WELL RECEIVED THAT I AM ENCOURAGED TO PRODUCE ANOTHER SERIES VIZ: "MORE AFRICAN PROVERBS"

IN THIS COLLECTION, THE NUMBER OF COUNTRIES OF ORIGIN OF THE PROVERBS IS INCREASED TO AS MANY AS TWENTY-FIVE.

All the proverbs remain as "Words of Wisdom" with their impact of philosophical, cultural and moral values.

It is my hope that "More African Proverbs" will be as well received and as much enjoyed as its predecessor "African Proverbs"

Lady Ademola
Lagos.

AMBITION

1

EVEN WHEN THE BIRD IS UP IN THE SKY,
ITS MIND IS ALWAYS ON THE GROUND.

Gambia

WHEN A HUNTER SETS A TRAP USING A
GOAT AS BAIT, HE DOES NOT EXPECT
TO CATCH A RABBIT.

Nigeria

THE HEN THAT PECKS ON A ROCK MUST
TRUST THE STRENGTH OF ITS BEAK.

Uganda

A BIG PLATE DOES NOT CONSUME A
LITTLE FOOD.

Zambia

AMBITION WITHOUT KNOWLEDGE IS
LIKE A BOAT ON DRY LAND.

Ghana

CHARACTER

4

FINE TREES BEAR JUICY FRUITS.

Botswana

NO MATTER HOW GOOD A DOG'S SUPPER IS, IT WILL STILL EAT GARBAGE.

Cote d'Ivoire

KOKODUS MEET KOKODUS AT THE FUNERAL OF A KOKODU; MEANING, BIRDS OF A FEATHER FLOCK TOGETHER.

Cote d'Ivoire

IF A MAN IS BORN IN A STABLE, HE
DOES NOT BECOME A HORSE, BUT IF
HE LIVES LONG IN THE STABLE, HE WILL
BEHAVE LIKE A HORSE.
Ethiopia

A BEE CAN NEVER BE AS SWEET AS
HONEY NO MATTER HOW LONG IT
STAYS IN THE BEEHIVE.
Gambia

A DONKEY CANNOT GET RID OF ITS
LARGE EARS MERELY BY SHAKING ITS
HEAD VIGOROUSLY.
Gambia

FINE COWS GIVE GOOD MILK.

Ghana

A CHILD WHO IS NOT TAUGHT WELL
AT HOME BY HIS MOTHER WILL BE
TAUGHT BADLY IN THE OUTSIDE
WORLD.

Guinea

IT IS OVER HONEY THAT THE
HONEYBEE BECOMES AGGRESSIVE.

Guinea

A CHAMELEON MAY CHANGE ITS COLOUR BUT IT DOES NOT CHANGE ITS NATURE.

Kenya

A HEN CAN NEVER LAY DUCK EGGS.

Nigeria

THE SIZE OF A CHICKEN DOES NOT LIE ON ITS FEATHERS.

South Africa

THE WAY A CAT WALKS IS NOT THE
WAY IT CATCHES RATS.
South Africa

NO MATTER HOW DARK IT IS, THE COCK
WILL ALWAYS KNOW WHEN TO CROW
AT DAWN.
Swaziland

A TWIG CAN NEVER BECOME A
CROCODILE, NO MATTER HOW LONG IT
STAYS IN THE RIVER.
Tanzania

He who would be a liar must have a good memory.

Uganda

It is a patient horse that does not stumble, and a patient wife who does not grumble.

Uganda

To learn to fly, a bird must first learn to leave the nest.

Zambia

10

THE MORE FEATHERS A CHICKEN HAS, THE BIGGER IT LOOKS.

Zambia

IT IS A FOOLISH COCK THAT CROWS AT DUSK.

Zimbabwe

A FROG NEVER JUMPS BACKWARDS.

Zimbabwe

NOT ALL THE TREES IN THE FOREST MAKE GOOD FIREWOOD.

Sudan

11

MILK IS EXACTLY THE SAME WHETHER
IT COMES FROM A BLACK COW OR A
WHITE ONE.

Tanzania

CONSEQUENCES

13

A DISEASE THAT WOULD KILL A DOG FIRST TAKES AWAY ITS SENSE OF SMELL.

Lesotho

A STONE THROWN IN RAGE SELDOM HITS ITS TARGET.

Malawi

DO NOT SWIM IN SHALLOW WATERS IF YOU DO NOT WANT YOUR BACK TO SHOW.

Malawi

A HEN THAT SWALLOWS A NEEDLE
WILL NOT LIVE LONG ENOUGH TO PREEN
ITSELF.
(Cameroon

IF YOUR FOOT SLIPS, YOU CAN
RECOVER YOUR BALANCE, IF YOUR
TONGUE SLIPS, YOU CANNOT RECOVER
YOUR WORDS.
Ghana

IF YOU DO NOT BRING FIRE NEAR A
TORTOISE, IT WILL NOT STICK OUT ITS
HEAD.
Ghana

WHEN THE GODS WANT A DOG TO DIE, THEY SIMPLY NUMB HIS SENSE OF SMELL.

Uganda

TO RUN AWAY FROM THE STINGS OF THE HONEYBEES, YOU MUST ABANDON THE HONEY.

Cameroon

WHEN YOU BRING INSECT-INFESTED WOOD INTO YOUR HOUSE, YOU INVITE LIZARDS IN AS WELL.

Cape Verde

Do not dig a hole for your enemy, for you do not know who may fall inside it.

Ethiopia

Those who refuse to drink from the well of knowledge will die of thirst in the desert of ignorance.

Guinea

The spoken word is like a stone, once it is thrown, it cannot be retrieved.

Ghana

You do not kill a calf in front of mother.
Kenya

He who refuses to obey cannot command.
Kenya

When two bulls fight, it is the grass that suffers. (Kenya)
The higher the monkey climbs, the more its buttocks are exposed.
Malawi

WHEN THE SEA DRIES UP, THE SUN
SHOULD SHARE IN ITS SHAME.

Ghana

IF A CHILD EATS SOUR FRUIT, IT IS THE
FATHER'S TEETH THAT ARE SET ON
EDGE.

Malawi

HE WHO WISHES TO PICK STONES
FROM THE BOTTOM OF A RIVER MUST
BE PREPARED TO GET WET.

Nigeria

19

An animal that eats thorns must know how to digest them in its stomach.
Nigeria

If you wish to gather honey, you must be prepared to risk the painful stings of the bees.
Nigeria

He who volunteers his head for the breaking of a coconut should not expect to eat from it.
Nigeria

HE WHO SELLS SAND AS SALT IS PAID
STONES AS MONEY.

Nigeria

HE WHO SETS FIRE TO HIS FATHER'S
HOUSE WILL INHERIT THE WRECKAGE.

Nigeria

IT IS ONLY WHEN AN EGG BREAKS THAT
YOU REALIZE THAT IT IS NOT ALL
WHITE.

Sierra Leone

21

CHICKENS THAT CACKLE TOO LOUDLY
WILL NOT HEAR THE HAWK COMING.
Sudan

THOSE WHO SOW THORNS SHOULD
NOT EXPECT TO REAP FLOWERS.
Swaziland

IF YOU ARE HUNTING A MAN-EATING
ANIMAL, BE PREPARED BECAUSE YOU
ARE BEING HUNTED YOURSELF.
Uganda

22

A TOAD WILL REALIZE THE
IMPORTANCE OF WATER ONLY WHEN
THE POND GETS DRY.

Zambia

A MAN WHO IS ACCUSED OF STEALING
GOATS SHOULD NOT ENTERTAIN HIS
GUESTS WITH DRIED MEAT.

Togo

23

CONTENTMENT

You cannot stretch your hands
further than the bones in them
will allow.

Cameroon

A tortoise for lack of vanity
carries its shell wherever it goes.

Zambia

DIFFERENT STROKES

26

THE PALM-WINE TAPPER IS LIKE A KING
TO A DRUNKARD.
Cameroon

THE ANTELOPE SAYS THAT HE IS NEVER
ANGRY WITH THE HUNTER WHO SHOT
AT HIM, BUT WITH THE DOG THAT
DROVE HIM FROM HIS HIDING PLACE.
Lesotho

A COCONUT SHELL FULL OF WATER IS
LIKE AN OCEAN TO A SMALL ANT.
Nigeria

If a dog chases a lizard in the rain, he should understand that his coat will remain wet long after the lizard is dry.

Namibia

Only when the cat is dead can the mouse lick its nose.

Zimbabwe

A team of pigs led by a lion is more formidable than a team of lions led by a pig.

Gambia

IF THE FLY SITTING ON TOP OF A
PALM-WINE CALABASH SAYS IT IS
DRUNK, WHAT WILL THE FLY INSIDE THE
CALABASH SAY.

Nigeria

EVEN AMONG ANTS, THERE ARE
GIANTS.

Nigeria

A DAY OF PEACE IN TIMES OF STRESS
IS LIKE A THOUSAND DAYS IN
PARADISE.

Nigeria

A WOMAN WORRIES ABOUT THE FUTURE UNTIL SHE GETS A HUSBAND, A MAN NEVER WORRIES ABOUT THE FUTURE UNTIL HE GETS A WIFE.

Uganda

30

DECEIT

31

WHEN A JACKAL WANTS TO CATCH A
SHEEP, IT DRESSES UP IN A LAMB'S
SKIN.

Lesotho

A SET OF WHITE TEETH DOES NOT
INDICATE A PURE HEART.

Nigeria

THE CAT WILL HIDE ITS CLAWS UNDER
ITS PAWS IN ORDER TO FEIGN
FRIENDSHIP WITH THE RAT.

Uganda

IF YOU WANT TO BURN DOWN YOUR
HOUSE, YOUR ENEMY WILL LEND YOU A
MATCH.

Zimbabwe

33

EXPERIENCE

34

When a child's groundnut is burnt in the fire, he eats the next one raw.

Uganda

You do not consult an oracle when you already know the cause of your illness.

Cameroon

A babe in its mother's womb does not feel the smoke in its mother's kitchen

Cameroon

35

New brooms sweep clean, but it is
the old ones that know all the
dirty corners.
Ghana

You don't touch what you
cannot see.
Kenya

If you know only one tune you
cannot dance all night.
Malawi

HE WHO SPLITS HIS OWN FIRE-WOOD
WARMS HIMSELF TWICE.

Malawi

IF YOU ARE TALLER THAN YOUR FATHER,
THAT DOES NOT MAKE YOU HIS PEER.

Malawi

HE WHO HAS NOT TASTED WHAT IS
BITTER WILL NEVER KNOW THAT WHICH
IS SWEET.

Sierra Leone

No matter how long the beard grows, it cannot compare itself in age with the eyebrow.

South Africa

He who sleeps on a mat knows the type of bug that bites him.

Tanzania

It is better to live in the corner of a roof than to share a larger room with a quarrelsome wife.

Uganda

THE EYES OF OUR ELDERS DO NOT
SHED TEARS FOR NO REASON.

Uganda

AN OLD MAN'S MOUTH MAY BE
TWISTED, BUT HIS WORDS ARE NOT.

Zambia

FORESIGHT

40

CROPS THAT ARE PLANTED ON A
HILLTOP WILL BE HARVESTED BY THE
WIND.
Cameroon

BEFORE YOU CUT DOWN YOUR
COCONUT TREE, CAREFULLY MEASURE
THE DISTANCE BETWEEN YOUR
NEIGHBOUR'S HOUSE AND THE TREE.
Cameroon

TAKE CARE NOT TO LOSE WHAT YOU
ARE HOLDING UNDER YOUR ARMPIT
WHEN TRYING TO HOLD ON TO THE
LOAD ON YOUR HEAD.
Ethiopia

A MAN WITH ONLY ONE ARROW TO HIS BOW SHOULD NOT SHOOT IT FAR FROM HOME.

Ghana

IF YOU LISTEN TO THE VOICE OF THUNDER YOU WILL NOT BE SOAKED WITH RAIN.

Ghana

A PERSON WHO HAS NOT SECURED A SPACE ON THE FLOOR SHOULD NOT LOOK FOR A MAT TO SPREAD.

Kenya

42

IF SOMEONE INTENDS TO ROAST YOU,
YOU DO NOT SMEAR YOURSELF WITH
OIL AND SIT BY THE FIRESIDE
AWAITING HIM.

Nigeria

A GIRL WHO GOES TO THE STREAM
EARLY IN THE MORNING FETCHES CLEAN
WATER.

Nigeria

A BEAUTIFUL PARROT THAT KNOWS
ITS FEATHERS ARE IN HIGH DEMAND
SHOULD NOT BUILD ITS NEST CLOSE TO
THE GROUND.

Nigeria

IF YOU SAY YOU WILL BREAK THE SKY WHEN YOUR FATHER DIES, STARTING CRACKING IT WHILE HE IS STILL ALIVE.

Sierra Leone

HE WHO SHOOTS AN ARROW UPWARDS TO THE SKY SHOULD HAVE HIS HEAD PROTECTED.

Sudan

A FARMER PLANTING HIS SEEDLINGS DOES NOT FEEL HAPPY LOOKING UP AT A CLOUDLESS SKY?

Uganda

NEVER FIGHT A STRANGER IN THE DARK, HE MAY TURN OUT TO BE YOUR BROTHER.

Zambia

A MAN WHO SITS BY THE BEACH WHERE FISHERMEN MAKE THEIR CATCH WILL NEVER EAT PLAIN RICE.

Zambia

FRIENDSHIP & LOVE

A smile is the strongest weapon
in the battle of life.

Ghana

Kind words do not wear out the
tongue.

Liberia

The only thing to do with good
advice is to pass it on.

Uganda

47

HARD WORK

IF A CHICKEN DOES NOT DIG, IT DOES
NOT FEED.

Cameroon

WATER FLOWING IN A RIVER DOES
NOT WAIT FOR A THIRSTY MAN.

Kenya

IT IS NOT NECESSARY FOR FINGERS TO
LOOK ALIKE, BUT IS NECESSARY FOR
THEM TO CO-OPERATE.

Kenya

49

YOU GAIN INTEREST ONLY ON WHAT
YOU INVEST.
Lesotho

IT IS BY GOING AND COMING THAT THE
BIRD BUILDS ITS NEST.
Ghana

IGNORANCE

51

BOWING DOWN TO SOMEONE DOES NOT MAKE YOU A SHORT MAN.

Nigeria

THE POISON THAT KILLS A DOG HAS LOST ITS SCENT.

Kenya

IF YOU GO INTO A FOREST TO LOOK FOR A PERFECT STICK, YOU WILL COME OUT EMPTY HANDED.

Liberia

THE MONKEY ON A TREE THAT EATS
WITH BOTH HANDS WILL FALL EASILY.
Sierra Leone

IF YOU DO NOT KNOW WHERE YOU
ARE GOING, ANY ROAD WILL TAKE YOU
THERE.
South Africa

IF YOU TELL A FOOL A PROVERB, HE
WILL ASK YOU TO EXPLAIN IT.
Zambia

FOLLOW THE RIVER AND YOU WILL
REACH THE SEA.
Ghana

NECESSITY

54

A hungry lion will make friends with a hyena.

Botswana

Though you wash your clothes with hot water, you still have to dry them in the sun.

Cameroon

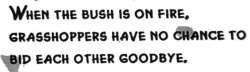

When the bush is on fire, grasshoppers have no chance to bid each other goodbye.

Kenya

HOWEVER TALL A TREE MAY BE, IT
CAN NEVER PREVENT THE SUN FROM
SHINING. (NIGERIA)

IT IS SURVIVAL NOT BRAVERY THAT
MAKES A MAN CLIMB A THORNY TREE.
Uganda

THOUGH YOU WASH YOUR CLOTHES
WITH HOT WATER, YOU STILL HAVE TO
DRY THEM IN THE SUN.
Cameroon

WHEN THE BUSH IS ON FIRE,
GRASSHOPPERS HAVE NO CHANCE TO
BID EACH OTHER GOODBYE.
Kenya

56

PATIENCE

A DOG CANNOT BITE AND BARK AT
THE SAME TIME.

Nigeria

THE WATER THAT YOU WILL DRINK
FROM THE RIVER WILL NOT FLOW PAST
YOU.

Nigeria

IF YOU WANT YOUR DINNER DONE, DON'T UPSET THE COOK. (ETHIOPIA)

CHANGING THE POT DOES NOT IMPROVE THE TASTE OF THE FOOD COOKING IN IT.

Ethiopia

A DOG CANNOT BITE AND BARK AT THE SAME TIME.

Nigeria

THE WATER THAT YOU WILL DRINK FROM THE RIVER WILL NOT FLOW PAST YOU.

Nigeria

THE YOUNG GOAT THAT RUSHES
WILDLY TO EAT LEAVES WILL ONE DAY
SWALLOW PRICKLY CATERPILLARS.

Nigeria

SELF CONTROL

MAKE SOME MONEY BUT DON'T LET
MONEY MAKE YOU.

Tanzania

SELF DELUSION

62

When the hen gets drunk, it forgets that the hawk exists.

Botswana

An elephant does not see the ticks on his own body but those on other elephants.

Botswana

The smallest beast in the bush is king in his own home.

Cameroon

DON'T CRY UNDER THE RAIN FOR YOUR TEARS WILL NOT BE SEEN.

Cameroon

A LAZY MAN BUILDS A HOUSE ONLY WITH HIS MOUTH.

Ghana

IGNORANCE MAKES THE RAT CHALLENGE THE CAT TO A FIGHT.

Kenya

YOU CANNOT CLIMB TWO TREES AT
THE SAME TIME JUST BECAUSE YOU
HAVE TWO LEGS.

Kenya

NOT EVEN A MAD MAN HAS A LOW
OPINION OF HIMSELF.

Kenya

A WISE MAN FOLLOWS THE ADVICE OF
HIS NEIGHBOURS BUT A FOOL TRUST
HIS OWN ILLUSIONS.

Mozambique

65

HE WHO IS ABLE TO RUN FROM HIS OWN SHADOW CAN ONLY COMMUNICATE WITH THE DEAD.

Namibia

NO ONE BARGAINS FOR YAMS THAT ARE STILL IN THE SOIL.

Nigeria

A CHICKEN FEELS SAFE AT AN EAGLE'S FUNERAL.

Sierra Leone

66

A FISH WEEPS BUT YOU DO NOT SEE ITS TEARS BECAUSE OF THE WATER THAT SURROUNDS IT.

Sierra Leone

THE MAN WITH A BIG NOSE THINKS EVERYONE IS TALKING ABOUT IT.

Sierra Leone

IF YOU DO NOT SEE ANYONE LOOKING AT YOU, DON'T CONCLUDE THAT YOU ARE NOT BEING SEEN.

Uganda

THE LAZY MAN BLAMES HIS POOR HARVEST ON WITCHCRAFT.

Uganda

DRUMS PLAYED IN THE NEXT VILLAGE SOMETIMES SOUND CLEARER THAN DRUMS PLAYED IN YOUR VILLAGE.

Zambia

IT IS NO USE OVER-FEEDING A PIG JUST BEFORE SLAUGHTERING IT BECAUSE YOU WANT TO EAT GOOD PORK MEAT.

Zimbabwe

TRUTH & HONESTY

YOU SHOULD NOT TRUST A MAN WHO SAYS THAT THE HIPPOPOTAMUS IS NOT AN UGLY ANIMAL.

Gambia

IT IS AN ILLNESS THAT CAN BE CURED, DEATH CANNOT BE CURED.

Guinea

HOWEVER HIGH YOUR SHOULDERS GROW, THEY CAN NEVER ATTAIN THE SAME HEIGHT AS YOUR HEAD.

Ghana

PEACE IS COSTLY BUT IT IS WELL
WORTH ITS PRICE. (KENYA)
IF A LEOPARD SELLS GOAT MEAT, FEW
PEOPLE WILL BUY IT.

Kenya

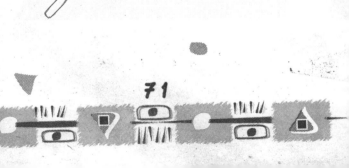

JUSTICE

72

WHERE THERE IS NOTHING TO LOSE,
THERE IS NOTHING TO FEAR.
Sudan

TO GET RID OF ANGER FIRST WEED
OUT THE BITTER ROOTS.
Zambia

NO ONE KNOWS WHAT GOES ON
BEHIND CLOSED DOORS.
Zimbabwe

UNITY

74

THE STRENGTH OF THE SOLDIER ANTS
LIES IN THEIR NUMBER.

Nigeria

THE FIRST CAMEL PULLS THE CARAVAN
BUT IT IS THE LAST THAT GETS THE
BEATING.

Sudan

IF YOU WANT TO KNOW HOW THE
HAND IS RELATED TO THE MOUTH,
SERVE YOURSELF A DELICIOUS MEAL.

Sudan

VIGILANCE

IF YOU ARE RIDING ON AN ELEPHANT,
DON'T FORGET THAT THERE MAY BE
SLIPPERY DEW ON THE GROUND.
Malawi

IF A FISH REFUSES TO OPEN ITS
MOUTH, IT DOESN'T GET CAUGHT.
Togo

WISDOM

YOU SHOULD NOT BEAT YOUR CHEST
WITH SOMEONE ELSE'S HANDS.

Cameroon

A MAN HUNTING AN ELEPHANT DOES
NOT STOP TO THROW STONES AT
BIRDS.

Cameroon

YOU DON'T THROW STONES AT A
FRUITLESS TREE.

Cameroon

IT IS NOT POSSIBLE FOR ONE FOOT TO CREATE A FOOTPATH.

Cameroon

A MONKEY THAT HOLDS THE BRANCH OF A TREE WITH BOTH HANDS DOES NOT EASILY FALL.

Gambia

IF YOU LOOK INTO AN EMPTY BOTTLE WITH TWO EYES, YOU ARE BOUND TO SEE WHAT IT CONTAINS.

Guinea

IT IS BETTER TO FLEE DANGER AND BE LAUGHED AT THAN TO FACE DANGER AND BE MOURNED.

Ghana

YOU DO NOT MEASURE THE DEPTH OF A RIVER WITH BOTH LEGS.

Ghana

EVEN THE LION, THE KING OF THE FOREST, PROTECTS HIMSELF AGAINST FLIES.

Kenya

PEOPLE WITH GRASS SKIRTS ON SHOULD NOT SERVE IN A FIRE BRIGADE.
Kenya

WHEN A RAT LAUGHS AT A DOG ITS HOLE IS NEARBY.
Nigeria

DO NOT THROW INSULTS AT A CROCODILE WHEN YOU ARE CROSSING A RIVER.
Nigeria

He who is surrounded by enemies should learn to sleep with one eye open.

Nigeria

An ant-hill that wants to survive should not grow mushrooms.

Sierra Leone

An ounce of experience is better than a pound of book knowledge.

Sierra Leone

TICKLE THE EARTH WITH A HOE AND IT
LAUGHS WITH A RICH HARVEST.
Sudan

DON'T ATTEMPT TO HIT A RAT THAT IS
STANDING ON A CLAY POT.
Tanzania

LOOK CAREFULLY WHERE YOU ARE
GOING OR YOU MAY END UP WHERE
YOU DO NOT WANT TO BE.
Zambia

You cannot sew a garment by moonlight.
Zambia

If a man wants to be friendly with wolves, he must first sharpen his spear.
Zimbabwe

Running water does not need a hole.
Gambia

85

A DOG WITH A BONE IN HIS MOUTH
DOES NOT BARK.
Ghana

A MAN WHO INHERITS HIS FATHER'S
WIDOW DOES NOT KNOW THAT BRIDE
PRICES ARE HIGH.
Ghana

IT IS NOT PROPER FOR THE KNEE TO
WEAR A CAP WHEN THE HEAD IS
AVAILABLE.
Ghana

IF YOU DO NOT KNOW HOW TO DANCE,
DON'T CALL A DRUMMER.

Ghana

THE INSECT THAT BITES YOU MAY BE
HIDDEN IN YOUR CLOTHES.

Ghana

THOSE WHO SPEAK TO YOU ABOUT
OTHERS WILL SPEAK TO OTHERS ABOUT
YOU.

Ghana

AN EGG HAS NO BUSINESS DANCING ON STILTS.

Ghana

IF PROBLEMS WERE LIKE MATS TO BE SPREAD, NO ONE WILL EVER NEED TO COMPLAIN.

Ghana

YOU CAN BLAME A MAN FOR PUSHING YOU DOWN, BUT YOU HAVE YOURSELF TO BLAME FOR REFUSING TO GET UP.

Ghana

A CORNFIELD THAT DOES NOT GROW
WEEDS IS SURELY NOT FIT ENOUGH TO
GROW CORN.
Ghana

WHEN A HANDSHAKE EXTENDS BEYOND
THE WRIST, AND THE ELBOW, IT IS NO
LONGER A HANDSHAKE, BUT A
WRESTLING MATCH.
Kenya

YOU CAN RECOGNIZE A CHILD WHO
FAILS TO TAKE ADVICE FROM HIS
BLEEDING WOUNDS.
Lesotho

TWO GOATS WITH LOCKED HORNS
CANNOT DRINK FROM THE SAME
BUCKET.

Liberia

UNLESS YOUR BACK IS BENT, NO ONE
CAN EVER RIDE ON IT.

Malawi

TWO BIRDS TIED TOGETHER,
ALTHOUGH THEY HAVE FOUR WINGS
CANNOT FLY.

Mauritius

90

It is the wind that tells the trees the kind of dance to dance.
Nigeria

The tortoise cannot make any progress until it sticks its neck out.
Nigeria

The bullet that kills an elephant is not as big as the elephant itself.
Nigeria

IF A CHILD CLAIMS TO BE TOO WISE,
GIVE HIM AN ANT TO SLAUGHTER.

Nigeria

PEACE AND INJUSTICE ARE LIKE DAY
AND NIGHT; THEY CANNOT STAY
TOGETHER.

Nigeria

A DOG DOES NOT EAT THE BONE HUNG
AROUND ITS NECK.

Nigeria

YOU DO NOT INQUIRE WHO IS
RESPONSIBLE FOR YOU FATHER'S
DEATH UNTIL YOU HAVE A SWORD IN
YOUR HAND.

Nigeria

UNTIL A ROTTEN TOOTH IS REMOVED,
ONE MUST CHEW CAREFULLY.

Nigeria

HOPE MAKES A GOOD BREAKFAST BUT
A BAD SUPPER.

Nigeria

93

DO NOT ARGUE WITH A MAD MAN
BECAUSE PEOPLE WATCHING WILL NOT
KNOW WHO IS WHO.
Nigeria

YOU DO NOT HAVE TO START A
DIALOGUE WITH A COW JUST
BECAUSE YOU WANT TO EAT BEEF.
Nigeria

A RABBIT THAT HAS ITS HOLE ON THE
FOOTPATH IS EITHER VERY BRAVE OR
IS A GOOD RUNNER.
Nigeria

94

IF YOU SEND SOMEONE WITH A BAG

OF SALT TO THE MARKET, DON'T SEND

A RAIN- MAKER AFTER HIM.

Nigeria

THE LAZY MAN IS DISGRUNTLED WHEN

THE COCK CROWS AT DAWN

HERALDING ANOTHER WORKING DAY.

Nigeria

THE VALUE OF PEACE IS NEVER KNOWN

UNTIL THE PEACE IS DISTURBED.

Sierra Leone

95

WHEN THE HAND GRINDS PEPPER, IT DOES SO TO THE DISADVANTAGE OF THE EYES AND NOSE.

Sierra Leone

WATER DOES NOT TURN DIRTY WITHOUT A REASON.

Sierra Leone

RESPONSIBILITY CAN ALSO CARRY BLAME.

South Africa

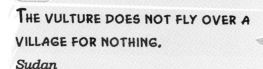

THE VULTURE DOES NOT FLY OVER A VILLAGE FOR NOTHING.

Sudan

THE MONKEY SWEATS BUT YOU DO NOT KNOW IT BECAUSE OF THE HAIR ON ITS BACK.

Swaziland

A DOCTOR WHO IS BALD TO THE NAPE OF HIS NECK CANNOT CURE BALDNESS.

Tanzania

It is easy to stand with a crowd, but it takes courage to stand alone.

Uganda

Short cuts may carry more traffic than the main road.

Uganda

A cockroach does not need to dress up to live in a king's palace.

Uganda

No matter how violent the wind may be, it can never force the river to flow backwards.

Zimbabwe

100